Flashes

Jennifer Firestone

Shearsman Books

First published in the United Kingdom in 2013 by
Shearsman Books
50 Westons Hill Drive
Emersons Green
BRISTOL
BS16 7DF

Shearsman Books Ltd Registered Office
30–31 St. James Place, Mangotsfield, Bristol BS16 9JB
(this address not for correspondence)

www.shearsman.com

ISBN 978-1-84861-225-9

To Butler Street

Flashes

Bowing down to this infrastructure
it is not just the name but history upon history
and you are the peon
it is very clearly demarcated
this is the bottom of the pile and no matter what
you should have your hand cupped
ready for overpourings.

We see bubbled wall in CHANCE
as a new addition
to neighborhood development
not bad old gentrification
instead we say together: beautification.
We are hot. Hotter. Red devils wagging our tails
steam from throats coating
observing trees.
We flip silver communicators
open our compacts
press our tiny palms
we're linked in one huge network
migrating gray upon gray.

We see morning flicker like the new egocentric.
We say orange is immediate.
We pile strappy objects, gloss our big skin
here we come to the wilderness
where everything is brick and stone
trees are really smaller infrastructures
transmitters, shiny poles concealing communications.
The flowers are people flying on bikes
the air is boxes lived in
and space is a word
until that itself is formed.

We add up how we're doing against the rest
and see the newest eatery or purchase the best sale item
as long as there's no malfunction and we're hydrated.
We stand proud and think of the guy with the ragged jeans
who declared in the interview: *my style—sweaty and hot*
and we think how figurative or literal this is supposed to be
but whatever he got the last image/word and we are in the field
hunting brightly colored eggs.

Revving up our power-bodies
we lift off to space
the fling of our motion leaves us grappling
for our own breathing valves.

Dumbfounded and dumber
we are late for employment
and all passages seem derailed.
If we buckle we can grasp a twanging pulsar
take a ride
meet our deadlines.

Ready for the first hot juncture. I glide slide walk on by.
Insinuating image in my fashionable walk.
Conceal my eyes
repeat repeat.

So much more livable when I'm barely dressed
and others are attached to chairs on sidewalks
temperature on forearms bristle.
So many ways to step down a street
to be noticed noticeable
to be the storekeeper's window.

Ways to hold a stem between which fingers and from what angle
interacting with the street lamp's light.

To not walk when stuffed, when willing to walk away from words
and be like cotton.
To see that decisions must be made on what is best.
When production's down
the idea of slowing is preposterous.

I send/sent the little message droopy bow and hope
through buzzing it receives gets received
and has with hope favorable outcomes.
The report flutters in that world
will be lit in one hour.
Fuzzy with fuzz, obedient.

When I text messaged you I insinuated help
and what will you eat this evening and
join me if you dare.

Others flipped open saw shrunken screen.
Some transferred images and then closed heart lockets.
Others hit 7 and erased others' languages.
Others hit 1 and then followed with many pushings.
Some jumped into bigger waters and
connected with other schools
said tap me into noises that can be recorded
deceive my everyday environment.

So there were dental drills and traffic sounds
and coughs to elicit illness.

Flowers at perimeters nestle
bees clinging sex upon sex wanting bulbs
the whole basket.
The flowers have an interior
rows and rows and then some
a myriad a mix of sorts
all pleasant outlines for the passerby.

Neighbor: I love I love your dark blood ruby what do you call them
they were here for weeks and then vanished
and many times I had to pause.

To go about these live things mutations
is what got me out of the house
to be working is always the right move
nail ripping is always the right place
for the ants to regroup motivate.

On the phone on a religious holiday a neighbor said: I am outraged
you have the audacity to discover I order the NY Times
this is an intrusion a misdemeanor of city laws
and she signed off the phone without a name
just a code, 2F.

Other neighbors don't mention: flowers, new garbage cans,
smell of rat, smell of spinach, the police, the Jehovahs,
the pot smoker, the actor/musician/coffee shop worker,
the documentarian and product placement photographer,
the PR person for the local politician.

Motorcyclists set off alarms
neighbor says: they must have small penises
gives her cigarette a puff.

When I asked where she was going she said why do you ask
she gave us a flier about her alarm system
that she emphasized was always on
and had the alarm company call to arrange a free consultation.

The windows never open some are without screens
and we can't find some that fit
or we did and it cost too much
and we'd rather have generated air.

Determined by where you grill your food
if you are on top and look down you are okay
and if you have a wall around your cooking you are better
you may have those surgically-equipped clamps and jabbers
to get good roasting done. But if you are at the bottom
you are in a lot with cans, cats and alcoholic beverages.
You are plastering the tar with frankfurters and forks.

Sadness sits on curves of letters and I figured
it's best to approach it head on.
I go back to this string from the bottom
yanked and plucked
no matter the object in front of one's face
it reverberates a slow moan or harp chord
as if to say rock the boat rock the boat
upset the torrent
this is not right something's happening
and I can't sit still.

A light goes off a spark plug
acting out.

Says:
three shot shots to three men on Friday evening
shot under umbrella of steel signage: CHANCE.

Says during garden-time hose slid
emerging green wetting everything.

It was thunder reminding me of three shots
by windows thickly hung
only then the hand tore one away and looked
to straight ahead other windows where fizzing light
and abundances of green, rained on green tangling up the fences
the heavy cat triggers its fall falling toward the plants
that decided to make it through time.

The screen is my friend though I want it to go away
the screen is perverse it wants to reel:
woman expecting killed was it fields was it woods
were there parts dragged onto earth.

There is talk of death and when and where.
The presidential body is in flight arriving soon
to an important location
where after allotted time
everyday beings will congregate.

Every channel doing its job every haircut placed among features.

The buildings block this building
so light between
is what I call mine
and if I am without clothes on the couch I feel I have the right
to show my body to the light and anyone who's watching.

I tune back and forth the antenna wobbles
disrupted by helicopters doing their evening sightings
the cameras go click and something shuts and pretends to nap
though overworking vigorously
just no production shown.

The screen said do you and I said I do. They in the background said
we did. And we all jumped
to black water.

The shark inside but I can't find it
I bait the hook with a bleeding minnow
but it's not enough for such strong teeth.

The shark knows about escape and tells me to move out
I have the wrong address attached to my persona
this is where the pot boils, the ticking tocks.

The shark's gone in a flurry
the rivulets of water curl away
coldly scolding he urinates in the stream
and it stings me
the yellow stench.

Bits of paper sparkled city, bits of skin tissued sidewalk
it was a sunny day   trees indicate so.

Downtown prayers arranged during morning breaks
sky inhabits purple light.
Thick quilted air felt on my legs
articles of clothing dampen
headlines in my head
instill the greatest fear
into a feeble human body.

Unpoured like animals from the ark we became friendly
like old days, we offered each other liquid
put away green bills, undid our jackets
clustered.

We approached a bridge, began to walk
we sang a railroad song, we chimed cow bells
we'd flown up the food chain from ants to big people
returning to our human states with our human faces.

He speaks: barbarians you will now cower
we are armed armored
do you know who you are up against
the biggest sports players in sequined jerseys
the biggest mouths with great dental hygiene
the biggest burgers good for the dollar
the best of all size does count.

He locates geographically evil areas
the little guy gets big
puts on black boots and is bad
examples lie freely.

He may be stiff not the rodeo contestant the wide-brimmed smiler
he may be tall his proportions easily imitable
a caricature awaiting
oh all shall pray.

He won't agree to talking one on one but lets nations collaborate
and develop group talk
and then will sign off on that.

He's got a horse to do some riding.

The cowboy torch passed one rough hand to another
Kick a bull in its balls.
Wild ones here we come.

Barbarians, thieves, uneducated, uncivil
why should a pact be held for such sects.
Need for new thinking in the law of war.

When writing about heroes you feel pride.
We galloped by his side. We said neigh I mean yay! The king is here.

Get away run while the creep turns his head.
Get to an alley hop the nearest transporter.
I am far in the middle
I'm starting to film.
Rolls go faster and faster by.

Shuffle to the music in the blank blank store
push my silver cage to dry goods.
Community holes have changed
and this no longer one of them.
Swipe the items home.

Electronic cards replace food stamps.
Should we say terror as in who's at my door.
What noise. Wings trimming sky.

He made a dollar more than her
in a store that saves us bucks.
Compliant or not it is what it is.
The terror not so terrible
when it's screening everyday.
I took the first flight home took
the flying lesson to be profound
about my own operation to own
leverage.

We barely talk about prospering land that is a little dying.
The birds call green but with a loss.
If my face touched I may go straight under
they'd poke a flag and say one lost life.

Despite birds scratching the branches
there is nothing happening.
I want a jolt, a blender action
I enter a long silver tube and jostle.
I'm wrapped in plastic
a well-wrapped item.
A voice alerts.
Elections are chortling
searching for slogans to be repeated recorded repeated
because they believe
only when necessary
and lots of brothers sisters sons gone dying here here here.

Are you listening screen
this about you and me living.
This is about god.
This is about heroism.
This is about no stars tonight.
This is about the heat that burst and continued.
This is a eulogy to the living.
This is an emotionless time.

Orange-draped hooded, they said cradled, cradles guns
the knife bouncing off protruded faces
the bump of sack on the ground
the bones on the ground.

Masterful plan of medieval torture
I watch the bowed men kneeling
reminded we too are remnants.
We dip with the first blunt stroke
wobble with the spinning top
let go.

The language detectives are out. Amphibious feet touch pad.
They make sure all words coil in worldly-filtered projections.

The language detectives are delighted.
That's right your mouth is moving in its rightful passage.

Red Alert:

The elite and the artists frustrate the others
have you seen the swath today
what rainbow are we in
who's doing the mural.

Downtime.
Others detect red pink shadows.
Time of new government
suits with badges somehow intrinsically connected
to new foundation.
Proudly, pinkly on the sidelines
watching tin mice running ground.

Another government can be modeled on all other masterpieces.
We will take a few steps the hokey pokey
flash our yellow teeth on the sidelines
holsters securely fastened.

New government alive and kicking
merits appointed to marching that one does.
The man, the III, really three I's.
We haunt this city
never mind we let some take their jewels.

Weather changes at a loss
tying bows on necks of trees.
Wind chill got the best of us.
When almost dead came in our ships
we used them till they really died.

Loosely thrown into sky.
This was not how things were supposed to be.
Because I don't really know what's happening there.
Because if I did know would it matter.

They jumped from building none noticed.
Flashy what does this flash card hold.
Concentration is at war and two young men wave their hands.
We value, the most for its value
without skin your meat is worth.

Soon I became oriented/aware of my city
I stopped ideas rolled into leaves
the lizard ran over my back
it was a nowhere-stopped state.

Yet what if I went to the end clung to the spines—
imagine city buildings a flash of blue coming through.

Acknowledgments

Excerpts from this poem first appeared in *580 Split, Alice Blue, BlazeVOX, Can We Have Our Ball Back, Dusie, Good Foot Magazine, HOW2, MiPOesias, Sonaweb* and *Xcp: Streetnotes.*

With thanks and appreciation to Dana Teen Lomax, Jill Magi, Eileen Myles, Sarah Rosenthal, Joanna Sondheim, Leni Zumas and especially, Jonathan Morrill.

The Author

Jennifer Firestone is the author of *Holiday* (Shearsman Books), and the chapbooks *Waves* (Portable Press at Yo-Yo Labs), *from Flashes* (Sona Books) and *snapshot* (Sona Books). She is the co-editor of *Letters To Poets: Conversations about Poetics, Politics and Community* (Saturnalia Books). She is an assistant professor of Literary Studies at the New School's Eugene Lang College. She lives with her family in Brooklyn.

Lightning Source UK Ltd.
Milton Keynes UK
UKOW031142271212

204111UK00001B/23/P

9 781848 612259